Let's Go!

Aubre Andrus

NATIONAL GEOGRAPHIC

Washington, D.C.

Vocabulary Tree

WAYS TO TRAVEL

VEHICLES

bike
car
bus
subway
plane

Let's go!

How?

There are so many ways!

Bikes are fun to ride.

They move when you do.
Pedal fast!

Helmets keep riders safe.

So do hand signals.
This one means "right turn." 9

Some people drive cars to get around.

Always use a seat belt!

Cars can be small.

Or they can be big.

Sometimes many people travel together.

Let's take a bus.
Wait for me!

Others like to ride the busy subway.

It's OK to stand, but
hold on tight. *Whoosh!*

Some people travel to places that are far away.

They can take a
plane to get there.

The plane flies above the clouds.

Look out the window!

Where do you want to go?

YOUR TURN!

Draw a picture of a place you want to go. What kind of vehicle will you take to get there: a bike, car, bus, subway, or plane?

For Mira. May you travel far. —A.A.

Designed by Anne LeongSon

The author and publisher gratefully acknowledge the literacy review of this book by Kimberly Gillow, principal, Chelsea Schools.

Photo Credits
Cover, anthonysp/Getty Images; 1, SimplyMui/Getty Images; 2-3, Monkey Business Images/Shutterstock; 4-5, Richard Nowitz/National Geographic Image Collection; 6-7, Sergey Novikov/Shutterstock; 8, Marilyn Nieves/Getty Images; 9, Marmaduke St. John/Alamy Stock Photo; 10, graphia/Shutterstock; 11, Africa Studio/Shutterstock; 12-13, B Christopher/Alamy Stock Photo; 14-15, Will & Deni McIntyre/Getty Images; 16, Matthew Ashmore/Alamy Stock Photo; 17, Kian Khoon Tan/Alamy Stock Photo; 18-19, pzAxe/Shutterstock; 20, IM_photo/Shutterstock; 21, maximkabb/Getty Images; 22, Sofie Delauw/Getty Images; 23 (LE), Léon Cherqaoui; 23 (RT), Mina Cherqaoui; 23 (markers), timquo/Shutterstock; 24, zenstock/Shutterstock; background art, hugolacasse/Shutterstock

Library of Congress Cataloging-in-Publication Data

Names: Andrus, Aubre, author.
Title: National Geographic readers. Let's go! / by Aubre Andrus.
Other titles: Let's go!
Description: Washington, DC : National Geographic Kids, [2019] | Series: National Geographic readers. Pre-reader | Audience: Age 2-5. | Audience: Pre-school, excluding K.
Identifiers: LCCN 2018035673 (print) | LCCN 2018049453 (ebook) | ISBN 9781426333378 (e-book) | ISBN 9781426333385 (e-book + audio) | ISBN 9781426333354 (pbk.) | ISBN 9781426333361 (hardcover)
Subjects: LCSH: Transportation--Juvenile literature. | Vehicles--Juvenile literature. | CYAC: Transportation. | Vehicles. | LCGFT: Instructional and educational works.
Classification: LCC TA1149 (ebook) | LCC TA1149 .A64 2019 (print) | DDC 388--dc23
LC record available at https://lccn.loc.gov/2018035673

Printed in the United States of America
19/WOR/1